HOW TO BE A
GREAT
STUDENT

HOW TO BE A
GREAT
STUDENT

The Ultimate Guide
for YOU to Learn, Prepare, and Become
the Best Student YOU Can Be

THOMAS ROBERTS

© 2007 Thomas Roberts

How to Be a Great Student: The Ultimate Guide for YOU to Learn, Prepare, and Become the Best Student YOU Can Be

All rights reserved. No part of this book may be used or reproduced in any manner whatsoever without permission.

Empower YOUniversity™ books may be purchased for educational, business, or sale promotional use. For information, please write Program and Projects Department, Empower YOUniversity, Post Office Box 3368, Merrifield, VA 22116.

Empower YOUniversity™ is a division of Roberts Education Corp™ and a member of the Great Student Network™.

Roberts Education Corp™, Empower YOUniversity™, and Great Student Network™ are trademarks of Roberts Education Corp.

First Edition

ISBN-13: 978-1-934616-55-0
ISBN-10: 1-934616-55-9

Empower YOUniversity

DEDICATION PAGE

*The two greatest gifts YOU can give
the student YOU care about are
unconditional love and a wonderful education.*

*This book is dedicated
with love, faith, and support*

To: _____

From: _____

Date: _____

Empower YOUniversity

*"Providing YOU the Fundamentals
to Win in the Game of Life"*

AUTHOR'S NOTE TO YOU

I fully believe that with the proper training, tools, time, and effort, YOU can learn whatever YOU desire. It is your willingness and ability to discipline yourself and persevere through the challenging times that will determine your success. Your commitment, determination, and internal desire to be the absolute best that YOU can be are ultimate drivers to your success.

This book provides training and tools to help YOU become a great student. But, the most important ingredients are up to YOU—time and effort. Regardless of how much others want to help YOU, no one can do it for YOU. Your success is up to YOU.

Do YOU want to be a great student? If so, put in the time and effort and become all that YOU can be.

YOU can do it!

Thomas Roberts

HOW TO USE BEGS

How to Be a Great Student is not just a book. It is a student's:

- Positive and helpful educational companion for life.
- Detailed road map for success in school.
- Comprehensive educational resource and training guide.
- Tailored support system.
- Personal tutor.
- Inspirational and motivational tool.

How to Be a Great Student is an action-based text that is designed to help YOU become a better student through a clear, simple, and easy-to-understand format, use of language, and structure. Each lesson is presented on its own page and then immediately explained and reinforced on the adjacent page in order to help YOU see the message, grasp and understand it quickly, and then explain "how to use" what YOU just learned and "why" that lesson is important for YOU to know and understand. The chapters are structured specifically to help YOU prepare for your first day of school through your final exams.

How to Be a Great Student was not written to be read once or memorized, then left on the shelf. It should be constantly reviewed, read, and considered. This book is a dynamic and interactive tool. To get the best results, YOU should:

- Skim the entire text before YOU concentrate on one particular lesson.
- Although the content is presented in the order in which it should be reviewed, focus on the lessons that YOU find most helpful and impacting to achieve immediate gains.

- Concentrate on one lesson at a time and a maximum of three per day.
- Digest and utilize the material in small bits.
- Read a lesson, practice it, and work to implement it into your school preparation.
- Practice the lesson YOU desire to learn repeatedly until YOU get it right and it becomes a positive study habit or behavior for YOU.
- Commit yourself to getting better.
- Work until YOU get it right.
- Maintain a positive, determined, and driven attitude throughout the process.
- Do not get deterred or distraught over mistakes.
- Be patient with yourself. Some of the lessons are easier to implement than others.

The best thing about this book is that it can always be with YOU. Keep it in your backpack. Whenever YOU need a refresher or reminder, pull it out, review the appropriate lesson, and get back on track.

If YOU learn, try, practice, develop, and implement the great study habits and behaviors in this book, YOU will become a better student.

TABLE OF CONTENTS

Chapter One:	Organizing for Class	1
Chapter Two:	Behaving in the Classroom	13
Chapter Three:	Dealing with Teachers and Educators	51
Chapter Four:	Being Resourceful	63
Chapter Five:	Focusing on Your Work	75
Chapter Six:	Learning How to Learn	85
Chapter Seven:	Preparing for Success	127
Chapter Eight:	Tackling Assignments and Homework	145
Chapter Nine:	Preparing for and Taking Tests	165
Chapter Ten:	Developing a Positive Learning Attitude	197
Chapter Eleven:	It Is Up to YOU!	233

CHAPTER ONE

Organizing for Class

Lesson #1

Get organized

Get organized

How?

- Use one notebook per subject.
- Print out your class schedule.
- Print out the school calendar.
- Chart all of your assignments on your personal calendar.

Lesson #2

Ask for the syllabus the first day of class

Ask for the syllabus the first day of class

Then what?

- If your syllabus is online, download it.
- Print it out.
- Skim the entire syllabus.
- Note all test, quiz, and essay dates.
- Note all homework assignments.
- Add all test and quiz dates, essay due dates, and assignment due dates to your personal calendar.
- Get the necessary books, CDs, and other materials.

Syllabus is the formal name for the complete schedule and listing of the topics, assignments, and due dates for a class. It is usually constructed by your teacher and distributed the first week of school.

Lesson #3

Make the most of your personal calendar

Make the most of your personal calendar

How?

- Chart all of your assignments on your personal calendar.
- Write down all tests and assignments on the appropriate day.
- Circle all test and assignment dates.
- Highlight the week before the test/exam, ending on the actual test/exam date.
- Begin to review and organize your notes a week before the test.

Lesson #4

Organize yourself

Organize yourself

- Get the proper school supplies such as pens, pencils, paper, notebooks, and a backpack.
- Create an organizational system.
- Keep track of your materials for school.
- Get organized with:
  - Notebooks
  - Computer/laptop
  - Calendar
  - Mobile device such as an MP-3 player or personal digital assistant (PDA)

Lesson #5

Organize your computer or notebook

Organize your computer or notebook

- Create a separate folder on your computer or use a separate notebook for each subject. Include:
  - Syllabus
  - All homework assignments
  - Essays and papers
  - Class notes

CHAPTER TWO

Behaving in the Classroom

Lesson #6

Go to school

Go to school

- Do not miss school.
- Attend all of your classes every day.
- Be on time!
  - It shows your commitment to your education and learning.
  - It is hard to do well when YOU miss how the information is originally presented by your teacher.
  - Missing school and class counts against YOU.
  - It is hard to learn when YOU are not around to hear what is being taught.

Lesson #7

Go to class

Go to class

- Be on time for class.
- Be fully present in the classroom.
- Pay attention to the class discussion.
- Show the teacher and your classmates that YOU are there to learn.
- Focus on your work, your teacher, and the lesson being taught.
- Keep your thoughts on the class, not "other things."
- Go to class to learn, listen, and participate.

Lesson #8

Participate in class

Participate in class

- Class participation is an important and sizeable portion of your grade.
    - Ask questions.
    - Answer questions.
- Participating in class shows everyone that YOU want to learn.
- It is a great way to practice, learn, and demonstrate what YOU have learned.
- It helps YOU develop a relationship with your teacher.
- It is a great way to get immediate help and feedback in areas where YOU need it.
- Class discussion typically covers and explains important topics, concepts, and questions regarding the material YOU are expected to learn.

Lesson #9

Sit in the front of the classroom

Sit in the front of the classroom

Why?

- It shows the teacher and your classmates that YOU are there to learn.
- It is easier to focus because only the teacher is in front of YOU.
- Seeing and hearing what is being taught, without obstructions or distractions, makes learning easier.
- YOU are less likely to be distracted by others when YOU sit at the front of the class.
- YOU are less likely to goof off and clown around when YOU are seated directly in front of the teacher.

Lesson #10

If your seat is not in the front, try these tips

If your seat is not in the front, try these tips

- Do not talk to the other students around YOU.
- Focus on what the teacher is saying.
- Concentrate on taking the best class notes that YOU can.
- Participate in class. When YOU participate, those around YOU have to behave better because your teacher is more aware of the activities around YOU.
- If other students are talking or distracting YOU, ask them to be quiet so that YOU can hear and learn.

Lesson #11

Conduct yourself with respect in the classroom

Conduct yourself with respect in the classroom

Why?

- To get respect, YOU must respect yourself first.
- YOU want to be taken seriously by your educators and classmates so:
  - Do not clown around.
  - Treat your pursuit of education with dignity and respect.
  - Speak with confidence and self-respect.
  - Come to class to learn and behave accordingly.

Lesson #12

Respect your classmates

Respect your classmates

How?

- Do not interrupt others.
- Do not talk while others are talking.
- Do not call anyone names.
- Do not tease another student.
- If YOU want respect, give it.

Lesson #13

Communicate directly with your educators about what YOU do and do not understand

Communicate directly with your educators

Never hesitate to ask for help when YOU feel confused or uncomfortable with the material or information YOU are trying to learn.

- Go directly to your educators when YOU need help.
- Be clear about the concepts that YOU do not grasp.
- Know that educators should provide YOU with suggestions, recommendations, and tools to help YOU learn whatever YOU are supposed to learn.

Lesson #14

Ask teachers what it takes to perform well in their classes

Ask teachers what it takes to perform well

Why?

- Provides YOU with helpful knowledge on what it takes to do well in your classes.
- Gives YOU another opportunity to establish rapport with your educators.
- Increases your educators' expectations of YOU, which should positively impact YOU.
- Helps YOU understand exactly what your teachers expect, like, and need from YOU in order for YOU to do well.

Lesson #15

Ask teachers for tips on learning their materials

Ask teachers for tips on learning their materials

Teachers can give YOU advice to make learning easier.

- This helps get the teacher to invest in YOU.
- These important tips and clues will make learning easier and help YOU perform better.
- Ask your teacher for specific suggestions on the various ways to learn the new material.

Lesson #16

Never show up an educator

Never show up an educator

- Even when wronged, praise in public, chastise in private.
- Be courteous and polite in front of others.
  - If YOU have something less than positive or serious to say to an educator, pull him/her aside first, then calmly and respectfully tell him/her.
- Do not embarrass an educator.
- Do not use foul language.
- Do not be rude or disrespectful to your educator.
- Do not yell at an educator.

Lesson #17

Take these steps if YOU have a problem with an educator

Take these steps if YOU have a problem with an educator

- "Widen the circle." Do not tackle the situation yourself.
- Tell your parent or caregiver first and ask for help.
- Tell your guidance counselor about the situation and ask for help.
- Ask the guidance counselor to accompany YOU in a conversation with the difficult teacher.
- If nothing improves, ask your parent or caregiver to go to school to speak with the teacher, guidance counselor, and principal.
- Remain respectful.
- Keep your emotions under control.

Lesson #18

Take these steps if YOU have a problem with another student

Take these steps if YOU have a problem with a student

- Ask the other student to stop harassing YOU.
- "Widen the circle." Do not tackle the situation yourself.
- Tell your guidance counselor about the situation and ask for help.
- Ask a teacher and your guidance counselor to accompany YOU in a conversation with the difficult student.
- Tell your parent or guardian what is happening.
- If nothing improves, ask your parent or guardian to speak with the principal about the situation.

Lesson #19

Take notes in class

Take notes in class

- Use organizational tools to keep your notes in order: get a separate notebook for each class or, preferably, a three-ring binder with pockets and tabs for each class.
- Write the date at the top of the first page of notes for each class period.
- Number the pages for each class session.
- Use bullets, headings, and indentions to organize your notes.
- Highlight or note important topics.

Lesson #20

Use these note-taking tips for better class notes

Use these note-taking tips for better class notes

- Listen attentively to what the teacher is saying.
- Write down the important themes, notes, and formulas that your educator emphasizes and writes on the board.
- Write the date and page number at the top of each page of notes.
- Write the important term or concept on the left side of the paper and then underline it.
- Write the definition, formula, or explanation underneath the important term.
- Skip a line between terms and themes.

Lesson #21

Listen with your eyes and your ears

Listen with your eyes and your ears

- Focus on the speaker.
- Watch the speaker.
- Listen to the speaker with a silent mind.
- Do not talk, look out the window, pass notes, or use e-mail during class.
- Pay complete attention to the educator leading the class.

Lesson #22

Ask questions and participate in class

Ask questions and participate in class

- Think.
- Probe.
- Seek further understanding.
- When YOU do not understand, ask the educator to clarify or explain. (Chances are, someone else in the class has the same question, too.)
- Answer questions when YOU know the answer.
- Positively contribute to the class.

Lesson #23

Dress appropriately for school and the classroom

Dress appropriately for school and the classroom

- Show that YOU respect yourself by dressing in a respectful manner.
- Wear your clothes in an orderly and neat fashion.
- Take off your hat inside the school building.
- Do not use headphones or cell phones in class.

CHAPTER THREE

Dealing with Teachers and Educators

Lesson #24

Always speak to and greet your teachers

Always speak to and greet your teachers

Why?

- The better your relationship with your teachers, the better your teachers will treat, help, and work for YOU.
  - Get to know your teachers.
  - Allow your teachers to get to know YOU.

Lesson #25

Ask your teachers and counselors for help— repeatedly if YOU have to

Ask your teachers and counselors for help

Why?

- YOU must own your future.
- YOU must own your education.
- YOU have rights at school.
- YOU deserve help.
- It is your educator's job, duty, and responsibility to respond to your request for help and help YOU learn.

Lesson #26

Develop a rapport with your teachers, counselors, coaches, and administrators

Develop a rapport with your educators

Developing a relationship with your educators is smart.

- Once on your side, educators can become great lifelong resources for YOU.

- When educators recognize that YOU genuinely want to learn and are committed to doing your best, they are more likely to invest in YOU.

- Once invested in YOU, educators are more likely to help YOU. It is human nature, as well as the duty of educators, to generously help those students who are positive and consistently putting in a tremendous effort to learn.

Lesson #27

Learn to spot the "helpers" in your school, regardless if he or she is your assigned teacher or not

Learn to spot the "helpers" in your school

Some people are more inclined to help than others. Helpers come in all forms, in all positions, and with various lessons to share. Find them, ask them for help, and keep your appointment.

- Look to learn from the people YOU interact with.
- Pay attention to the positive and generous helpers around YOU. Get to know who they are.
- Develop an ability to locate the positive helpers in your school, community, and environment.
- Ask them for help.
- Be specific about your needs and concerns.
- Listen carefully to their response.

Lesson #28

Ask your teacher: "What can I do to earn extra credit?"

Ask your teacher: "What can I do to earn extra credit?"

Why?

- Boosts your grade.
- Helps demonstrate your willingness and desire to perform well.
- May help YOU offset a poor performance on an assignment.
- Gives YOU another opportunity to practice, which will help YOU learn.

CHAPTER FOUR

Being Resourceful

Lesson #29

Learn what resources and services are available to help YOU

Learn about available resources and services

Each school system and state board of education has a website that contains a list of the available programs and requirements to inform and assist students and parents throughout the educational process.

- Visit and review these websites.
- Learn your school's rules.
- Learn the specific criteria necessary to advance or graduate—specifically: the classes, grade point average, and activities.
- Learn what programs, resources, and services are available to help YOU do better in school.
- Familiarize yourself with the free tools, training, and support that are provided through your school or school district.

Another source: Ask your guidance counselor to provide YOU with all of the relevant school and school system rules, regulations, and information.

Lesson #30

Interview the good students in your grade and the grade above YOU

Interview good students

- Ask questions about:
  - Teachers
  - Classes
  - Workload
  - Schedules
  - Types of challenges
  - Any suggestions
  - Any warnings
  - Study skills recommendations
- Listen to their responses carefully.
- Learn as much as YOU can from their experiences and perspectives.
- Determine what information is most relevant or similar to your situation.
- Learn from their successes and failures. Ask them what worked well and what to avoid.

Lesson #31

*Familiarize yourself
with the various sources
of assistance
in your community*

Familiarize yourself with sources of assistance

- Federal, state, and local departments of education
- Federal, state, county, and district educational websites
- Parent Teacher Association (PTA)
- Non-profit organizations
- Religious groups
- Community organizations
- Supplemental educational services
- Tutor services
- Learning centers
- Local colleges or universities
- Online programs

Lesson #32

Use the Internet wisely and with discipline

Use the Internet wisely and with discipline

Search engines such as Google®, Yahoo!®, and Wikipedia® bring the world to your fingertips in seconds.

- Use the Internet as a learning tool.
- Type in keywords when searching to help YOU find relevant website links.
- Use quotation marks around a keyword to narrow down your search.
  - Example: Type "Great Student Network" in the search engine of your choice and notice how more accurate links are presented for your search.

Lesson #33

Check out your public library— it's an awesome place!

Check out your public library—it's an awesome place!

Get your library card today!
- Using the library is free.
- It is open and accessible to everyone.
- Most libraries have computers that can be used for free.
- YOU can read books, rent movies and CDs, and skim periodicals from all over the globe.
- The library is a great place to broaden your horizons and explore the world.
- Libraries also have training courses (computer, reading, education, etc.) for little to no cost!
- Libraries are quiet, peaceful, and safe places to go.
- Become an expert in all of the activities, services, and programs at your local library.

CHAPTER FIVE

Focusing on Your Work

Lesson #34

Focus on learning all that YOU can

Focus on learning all that YOU can

Why?

- When YOU focus on learning versus making the grade, YOU have a better chance of actually retaining and using the material.

How?

- Learn; do not just memorize.
- Concentrate.
- Attempt to understand the material well enough to be able to explain it correctly to someone else.

Lesson #35

Turn off your MP-3 player, CD player, and TV

Turn off your MP-3 player, CD player, and TV

- Study, read, and work without distractions, extra noise, sounds, music, or television.
- Learn to prepare with total concentration and without distractions.

Why?

- Enables YOU to focus solely on what YOU are working on.
- Increases your ability to remember, retain, and understand what YOU are trying to learn.
- Improves your ability to concentrate on your work.

Lesson #36

Learn to focus solely on what YOU are doing at that time

Learn to focus solely on what YOU are doing at that time

How?

- Read with a clear head.
- Turn off music and the television.
- Minimize distractions by seeking a quiet place such as the library.
- Slow down.
- Concentrate.
- Think solely about the work YOU are completing at that time.

Lesson #37

Focus on being able to think

Focus on being able to think

- Develop your ability to think.
- Practice.
- Evaluate your performance.
- Determine how and when YOU learn and think best.
- Challenge yourself to focus on one topic at a time.
- Work to ignore all distractions.
- Commit to fully concentrating on the one thing that YOU are working on.

CHAPTER SIX

Learning How to Learn

Lesson #38

Find out what kind of learning works for YOU

Find out what kind of learning works for YOU

- Learning is a process and a skill.
- People approach learning differently.
  - Learn what works best for YOU.
  - Be open to and try various methods of learning.
- There are multiple types of intelligence:
  - Visual or spatial
  - Verbal or linguistic
  - Logical or mathematical
  - Bodily or kinesthetic
  - Musical or rhythmic
  - Interpersonal
  - Intrapersonal

Source for "multiple types of intelligence":
www.ldpride.net/learningstyles.MI.htm

Lesson #39

Learn the material as YOU go; don't simply "memorize" it

Learn the material as YOU go

Why?

Learning the material as YOU go is better than memorizing or cramming for tests.

- Makes it easier to prepare for tests, quizzes, or exams.

- Relieves the pressure from having to learn all new information in large amounts.

- Makes each new lesson easier to follow because YOU are working and learning at the same pace that the teacher is working.

- Helps YOU "know" the material so YOU can use it whenever YOU need to.

- Makes it easier to learn new concepts. Most new concepts are built on previous lessons. Learning material as YOU go creates a foundation for grasping new concepts.

- Makes the class discussion more relevant and helpful as it works to reinforce and clarify what YOU are attempting to learn.

Lesson #40

Keep up with all reading assignments

Keep up with all reading assignments

Why?

- It is easier to learn in small bites.
- YOU can learn as the teacher instructs the class.
- YOU do not fall behind.
  - Once behind, it is hard to catch up.
  - Once behind, your emphasis becomes catching up versus learning what YOU actually read.

Lesson #41

Master the basics first

Master the basics first

Why?

- It is easier to learn in small bites.
- Learning is cumulative.
- Most lessons are organized as building blocks.
  - Learning and mastering step one is critical to learning and understanding step two and the subsequent steps.
- Learning becomes difficult once YOU fall behind.
  - It is hard to catch up.
  - It adds tremendous pressure and stress, which both inhibit learning.

Lesson #42

Teach and help others

Teach and help others

Why?

- If YOU can explain the material in detail and with comfort to someone else, then YOU actually know and understand the subject matter.
- It provides YOU with practice.
- It builds confidence.
- It allows for repetition, which will help YOU retain what YOU learned.
- It aids in your own learning and understanding.

Lesson #43

*Read it,
write it down,
then read what
YOU wrote aloud*

> **Read it, write it down, then read what YOU wrote aloud**

Why?

- This process improves your ability to retain the material.
- The more YOU do this, the easier it will become for YOU to remember and learn your material.
  - Focus on each step.
  - Repeat and practice.

Lesson #44

*Use note cards
to help YOU study*

Use note cards to help YOU study

How?

- Write the topic, definition, formula, or word YOU are trying to learn on one side of a standard note card.

- Write the appropriate definition, explanation, or formula steps on the back of the card.

- Review the note cards repeatedly—until YOU can recite the correct answer without looking at the back of the card.

Lesson #45

Use the "folded paper system" to help YOU study

Use the "folded paper system" to help YOU study

The "folded paper system" is similar to the note card system. Instead of using note cards, YOU create a study aid out of a sheet of paper. Here's how:

- Fold a piece of paper in half lengthwise.

- Open the paper. At the top of the left side, write "Topic/Question." At the top of the right side, write "Definition/Answer/Formula."

- Write the topic/question in the "Topic/Question" column.

- Write the definition/answer/formula opposite the topic/question in the "Definition/Answer/ Formula" column.

- Read the topic or question.

- Read the definition or answer.

- Repeat each step twice.

- Then attempt to recite the correct answer without looking at the right side of the page.

Lesson #46

Use highlighters

Use highlighters

- Highlight important topics, themes, and terms, but not the entire page.
- Focus on the information that the teacher indicates is important for your class.
- Develop your own system that helps YOU identify then retain important information.
- Review the material YOU highlight routinely.

Note: Before YOU highlight in any school textbooks, make sure YOU have the school's permission.

Lesson #47

Be aware that there are different types of understanding

Be aware of different types of understanding

There are two types of understanding: 1) being able to explain a process, and 2) just being able to provide an end result or final answer. For example, think of a watch.

Process: How does the watch work?

- To answer this question correctly, YOU must know and explain the underlying components, processes, and attributes of the watch in addition to knowing how to tell time.

- It involves mastering and understanding the comprehensive, meticulous, and detailed processes and components of what is being taught.

- At times, a teacher will require YOU to know not only the final answer, but be able to explain all of the steps in the process to getting the answer.

Just the answer: What time is it?

- To answer this question correctly, YOU must merely know how to tell time.

- The teacher merely wants YOU to provide the correct answer, not the data or processes that led YOU to the correct answer.

HOW TO BE A GREAT STUDENT

Lesson #48

Learn from your mistakes— ALWAYS!

Learn from your mistakes—ALWAYS!

Mistakes are part of the process. How do YOU learn from your mistakes?

- Carefully review all of your exams, papers, and assignments after they are corrected by your educator.
- Review what YOU got correct and what YOU got wrong.
- Examine the questions YOU missed and learn why YOU missed them.
- Correct your mistakes, remember the answers, and then do not make the same mistakes again.

Lesson #49

Create a "study group"

Create a "study group"

- Find friends to review and discuss each day's lesson.
- Pull together a group of peers—a study group—to help prepare for exams.
- Get help from peers that understand the material.
- Offer to assist others who need your help as well. Teaching others is a great way to retain and strengthen your grasp of new material.

Lesson #50

Review your class notes at the end of each day for each class

Review your class notes at the end of each day

- Skim your notes every day for each class.
- Put question marks by everything that YOU do not understand.
  - Ask your educator about it in class the next day or e-mail your teacher your question.
- To excel, rewrite your notes every day.
  - Date each set of class notes.
  - Focus on important topics, themes, and concepts.
  - Write legibly and clearly.
  - Review your rewritten notes once YOU have completed them.

Lesson #51

Learn how to be a "good listener"

Learn how to be a "good listener"

- Listen and hear what the educator is saying.
- Focus on what he or she is saying, writing, and doing.
- Keep a clear head and a silent mind.
- Maintain eye contact with educators.
- Listen with a smile.
- Acknowledge the speaker (with a slight nod) to let him or her know that YOU are paying attention.
- Sit up in your chair or desk. Do not slouch.
  - Your body language communicates whether YOU are truly engaged or listening more than YOU realize.

Lesson #52

Read things that YOU enjoy in your spare time

Read things that YOU enjoy in your spare time

- It provides YOU with an opportunity to practice.
- It will improve your ability to read.
- It will help YOU learn new things about topics that interest YOU.
- It is a fun way to improve your ability to learn.
- It will help YOU become more comfortable with your ability to read.
- It is a fun way to develop and practice your reading skills.

Lesson #53

Discuss what YOU are learning with others

Discuss what YOU are learning with others

- A great way to learn and retain anything is to educate others.

- Talking about your work will help YOU to better absorb and remember what YOU are attempting to learn.

- Teaching others will not only help YOU learn better, but it will enable YOU to feel better because YOU are helping someone else.

Lesson #54

Increase your confidence with learning

Increase your confidence with learning

- Every time YOU learn something new—big or small—YOU have accomplished something.
- The more things YOU learn, the more confident YOU will become in your ability to learn new things and to put your knowledge to work in your life.
- Learning is a habit. The more YOU do it, the better YOU will become at it.

Lesson #55

ALWAYS ask questions when YOU don't understand what is being taught or explained

ALWAYS ask questions when YOU don't understand

- Most times, YOU are not the only person to have that exact question. Therefore, YOU are clarifying a question for others as well as yourself.
- YOU only hurt yourself when YOU fail to ask for the help that YOU need.
- If educators do not know YOU need help, chances are YOU will never get it!
- Put your fear aside and ask your questions. If YOU are afraid to ask a question out loud:
  - Ask the teacher after class.
  - Send the teacher an e-mail that contains the question.
  - Jot the teacher a quick note with the question on it.

Lesson #56

Create "summary sheets" to help YOU study

Create "summary sheets" to help YOU study

A "summary sheet" is a worksheet or study aid that YOU create. It summarizes your notes, lessons, and assignments. Here's how YOU create one:

- Summarize your notes, lessons, and assignments on a piece of paper.
- Write down the core themes/formulas and the important components that support those themes/formulas.
- Write down all important words, terms, and themes and their definitions.
- Review the material several times before YOU take your test.

Lesson #57

Use initials to help YOU remember important material

Use initials to help YOU remember important material

When YOU use initials to help YOU remember material, they are called acronyms. Here's how YOU create and use acronyms:

- Simplify the material so that YOU can best remember it.
- Utilize the first initial of the words or process that YOU need to recall.
  - Example: What colors are in the American flag? Remember: "RWB."
    Answer: "RWB," which stands for red, white, and blue.
- Repeat and practice until YOU know your material.

HOW TO BE A GREAT STUDENT

CHAPTER SEVEN

Preparing for Success

Lesson #58

Learn how to prepare

Learn how to prepare

- Get organized.
- Determine what is expected from YOU.
- Look at the syllabus and class schedule.
- Know when all tests and assignments are scheduled or due.
- Do your work on time.
- Complete practice problems.
- Review your notes.

Lesson #59

Ask for additional work and do it

Ask for additional work and do it

- It lets your educators know that YOU:
  - Are serious about learning.
  - Are willing to do the extra work to learn.
  - Want and expect their help.
- It also gives YOU an opportunity to practice.
- Again, more practice means more preparation, which leads to increased confidence, which will result in better performance.

Lesson #60

*Always do
the extra problems*

Always do the extra problems

Why?

- The more problems YOU complete the better YOU will be able to handle test questions.
- YOU will gain confidence from having success in practice.
- Errors in the extra work will help YOU see where YOU need to get help to correct your mistakes.
- Many times, the test/exam questions mirror the extra problems.

Lesson #61

Take practice tests or quizzes repeatedly

Take practice tests or quizzes repeatedly

Why?

Practice tests and quizzes help YOU to:

- Learn how the teacher asks questions.
- Practice and reinforce your learning.
- Gain confidence in your knowledge and understanding.
- Remove fear and doubt about your ability to perform well on the actual test.
- Expose yourself to the various ways that YOU could be tested on the material.

Lesson #62

Constantly seek feedback

Constantly seek feedback

- The best way to get the feedback YOU need is to ask for it. Ask:
  - What could I do better?
  - How can I improve?
- The more often YOU seek feedback, the more likely the educator will realize that YOU are serious about your pursuit of knowledge.
  - Listen calmly to the feedback.
  - Try to understand how YOU can use the feedback to improve your learning and your performance.
  - Incorporate the feedback into your study habits and routine.

Lesson #63

Practice

Practice

The only way to get better at anything that YOU do is to do it repeatedly.

- Practice enables YOU to get better!
- Practice gives YOU the opportunity to learn and grow from your mistakes.
- Practice builds confidence.
  - Confidence comes from knowing that YOU can do it.
  - Your confidence grows as YOU begin to answer questions correctly.
  - Your confidence also increases because YOU are likely to have a test question that is similar to the practice questions—and YOU have already answered those correctly.

Lesson #64

Find a regular place to study and work

Find a regular place to study and work

- Create a routine for studying.
- Let people know that your special study area is a "learning zone" only.
- Ask family and friends to respect the learning zone by being quiet and peaceful.
- Develop comfortable and regular study habits.
- Pick a place where YOU can focus, study, prepare, read, write, and think.

Lesson #65

Get your rest on school nights, especially before tests, quizzes, and exams

Get your rest on school nights

Why?

- YOU perform better when rested and calm.
- YOU are able to think better when YOU are not sleepy, tired, or worn down.
- YOU are less likely to fall asleep or "zone out" when YOU have received the proper rest.
- YOU will perform and learn better because YOU are more alert and energetic.

CHAPTER EIGHT

Tackling Assignments and Homework

Lesson #66

Do your homework before YOU do anything else when YOU get home from school—no exceptions!

Do your homework before YOU do anything else

- It provides YOU with a great opportunity to review your work and correct errors with a fresh mind after YOU have completed other tasks or activities.
- YOU ensure that YOU always get your work done.
- It protects YOU from running out of time "later."
- YOU work with a better focus, energy, and less pressure.
- YOU will be able to enjoy the rest of your day without negative feelings about the work YOU still have to do.
- If YOU have any questions, YOU will be better able to ask someone to help YOU before it gets too late in the day.

Lesson #67

Establish a successful homework habit

Establish a successful homework habit

- Remember that success comes from building good habits.
- Establish a routine.
- Set a time every school night for studying only, regardless if YOU have an assignment due the next day or not.
- Discipline yourself to study and review your work every day.
- Ask others to respect your study time by not disturbing or distracting YOU during the allotted time.
- Become an expert in learning. Since learning is a process, the more YOU practice and prepare, the better YOU will become at learning.

Lesson #68

Read with a pen or pencil

Read with a pen or pencil

Why?

- Helps YOU note where the important topics are.
- Makes it easier to find important material.

How?

- Write keywords at the top of the page.
- Write in the margin.
- Underline key terms and passages.
- "Block" passages then note with a comment or term to describe the lesson of the passage.

Note: Before YOU write in any school textbooks, make sure YOU have the school's permission.

Lesson #69

Always double-check your work

Always double-check your work

Why?

- YOU will catch any careless mistakes.
- It is a great habit to verify your answers.

How?

- Verify that the letters match in multiple-choice questions.
- Check spelling.
- Make sure YOU answered all of the questions.
- Verify that your math is correct.

Lesson #70

Read all that YOU can

Read all that YOU can

Why?

- Practice makes perfect.
- It helps YOU learn how to learn.
- It improves your ability to read, retain, and understand.
- The more YOU read, the easier reading becomes.
- The better reader YOU are, the more confidence YOU will develop.

Lesson #71

When reading, skim the material first to see the themes

When reading, skim the material first to see the themes

- Review the table of contents, chapter list, and section headers to see what YOU are about to learn.
- Read with a pencil or highlighter.
- Look for information that describes or supports the central themes.
  - Identify important topics and themes by the chapter titles and section headings.
- Note (underline or highlight) facts or important assertions.

Note: Before YOU write in any school textbooks, make sure YOU have the school's permission.

Lesson #72

Prepare an outline before YOU write essays

Prepare an outline before YOU write essays

- Write the central theme at the top.
- List important facts, quotes, or data underneath the theme to support it.
- Only begin writing after YOU have created a road map first.
- Construct a draft by making sentences from the information YOU used to construct your outline.
- Set the draft aside for one day and re-read it tomorrow.
- Review what YOU wrote, correct the errors, and set aside for one more day.
- Repeat the previous step one more time.

Lesson #73

The only way to get better at math is to do the problems—PERIOD!

The only way to get better at math is to do the problems

Practice and repetition will help YOU score better, perform better, and more easily grasp math concepts.

- Do the work!
- Do as many practice problems as possible.
- Learn each step in the math solution process.
- Show your work (each step) when YOU complete your math work.
    - It will help YOU grasp each step of the process.
    - Your teacher can see your thought process.
    - Your teacher can more easily see what YOU do and do not understand.
    - It could mean higher scores, if your teacher gives partial credit for using the process correctly even if your final answer is wrong.
- Review each problem and learn from what YOU did right and what YOU did wrong.

Lesson #74

Turn your work in on time

Turn your work in on time

YOU lose points for late work, so turn in all of your assignments by the due date—no excuses, no exceptions. Why throw away points? The best way to learn and improve is by doing the work.

- Answer every problem and question.
- Learn from your efforts.
- Correct the mistakes.
- Remember the successes.
- Whenever possible, keep and review your graded assignments. They are a great tool for studying and practicing.

CHAPTER NINE

Preparing for and Taking Tests

Lesson #75

When preparing for tests, anticipate or guess what the teacher expects YOU to know, understand, and be able to do

Anticipate what the teacher expects YOU to know

How?

- Look at the homework assignments, quizzes, and featured topics.
- Review the syllabus for important topics.
- Review previous tests or practice problems.
- Note the chapter titles and review questions from your textbooks and assignments.

Why?

- Improves your chances to perform well because YOU are well prepared.
- Improves your confidence because YOU have familiarized yourself with the important material that YOU have covered in class.

Lesson #76

Slow down during tests

Slow down during tests

- Read the directions carefully.
- Read each question fully.
- Take your time.
- First, eliminate answers that do not make sense—then consider the others.
- Focus on what is in front of YOU.
- Answer each question on the test, even if YOU have to guess.

Lesson #77

Prepare properly for tests and avoid cramming

Prepare properly for tests and avoid cramming

Why?

- If YOU study properly, YOU will not have to cram.
- Cramming for tests makes YOU more stressed out, which interferes with your ability to perform.
- YOU do not retain or remember most of what YOU cram anyhow.
- Learn the material as YOU go and make the effort to properly prepare.

Lesson #78

Prepare for your test with a set routine

Prepare for your test with a set routine

How do YOU prepare for a test?

- Begin your review and test prep early, preferably, at least one week before your test date.
- Review and organize your notes from the class.
- Review your old tests and quizzes from the class.
- Review all homework assignments.
- Create and review your summary sheets, note cards, and paper folds.
- Anticipate the questions that your teacher will likely ask YOU.
  - Pay special attention to the topics and problems that were common across all assignments.
  - Ask: What does your educator expect YOU to know?
- Do as many practice problems, tests, and quizzes as YOU possibly can.
- The night before a test: Get your rest so YOU can do your best.

Lesson #79

Review your summary sheets

Review your summary sheets

- Review your summary sheets several times before YOU take your test.
- Learn what is on your summary sheet.
- Remember what is on the sheet.
- Quiz yourself as practice for the tests.
- Be able to recite what is on the summary sheet without looking at it.

Lesson #80

Make sure YOU have the proper tools on exam days

Make sure YOU have the proper tools on exam days

- Be prepared mentally and physically on test days.
- Have the proper paper and writing utensils (a working pen or pencil) with YOU.

Why?

- Allows YOU to completely focus on your exam.
- Removes worry and stress about unnecessary things.

Lesson #81

If YOU run out of time to properly prepare and YOU have to study at the last minute, remember these tips

If YOU run out of time to prepare, try these tips

- Make summary sheets, paper folds, or note cards for the most important topics from your syllabus.
- Review all of your class notes.
- Review all graded assignments.
- Pay extra attention to the quizzes, homework assignments, and practice problems.

Lesson #82

Learn the various test types

Learn the various test types

- Teachers test what YOU have learned in various ways.
- Each method requires different approaches.
- The various test types are:
  - Multiple choice
  - Essay
  - True or false
  - Fill in the blank
  - Short answer
  - Matching

Lesson #83

*Multiple-choice tests:
Be sure to read the questions
and answers carefully*

Multiple-choice tests: Read the questions and answers

Tips for taking multiple-choice tests:

- Carefully read each question first.
    - Usually, there are four choices per question.
- Immediately eliminate answers that do not make sense.
    - Typically, two answers do not make sense, while the other two answers could be right.
- From the remaining answers, select the answer that best answers the question.
    - Look for the keyword or phrase that most directly and correctly addresses the question asked.

Lesson #84

Essay tests: Gather then organize your thoughts

Essay tests: Gather then organize your thoughts

Tips for taking essay tests:

- Read the directions and the question carefully.
- Take a minute to gather your thoughts.
- On the back side of the test or a separate sheet of paper, jot down all of the important facts, quotes, and data that are relevant to the question.
- Then, organize your essay with the following paragraph format:
  - Opening introductory sentence or statement
  - Core sentences that support your opening sentence and that include the relevant data, quotes, and facts
  - Conclusion
- Repeat with solid transitions between paragraphs until your essay is complete.

Lesson #85

*True-or-false tests:
Use common sense*

True-or-false tests: Use common sense

Tips for taking true-or-false tests:
- Read each question carefully.
  - What is the question asking YOU?
  - Which answer makes the most sense?
  - What word or phrase makes the statement true?
  - What word or phrase makes the statement false?
  - What word or phrase would make the statement true?
  - What word or phrase would make the statement false?

Lesson #86

Fill-in-the-blank tests: Look for information in the question to help YOU

Fill-in-the-blank tests: Look for info in the question

Tips for taking fill-in-the-blank tests:

- Carefully read each question.
- Look for information in the question to help YOU remember or understand what words best fit in the blank.
- Think back to your homework, class notes, and various assignments for important terms or concepts during the school year.

Lesson #87

Short-answer tests: Answer the question directly with facts

Short-answer tests: Answer the question directly

Tips for taking short-answer tests:

- Read each question carefully.
- Jot down your thoughts on important facts and information regarding the question.
- Write the facts in short sentences that directly address the question.

Lesson #88

Matching tests: Pair the questions and answers YOU know belong together first

Matching: Pair the questions and answers YOU know

Tips for taking matching tests:

- Skim the terms/questions on the left side first.
- Identify the terms YOU know right away.
- Answer those questions first.
- Locate the answer or definition that corresponds to that question or term.
- Write the number or letter that matches the term in the appropriate space.
- Cross off the number or letter immediately after YOU use it to eliminate that response from further consideration as a possible answer to another term/question.

Lesson #89

Take an SAT or an ACT standardized testing preparatory course before YOU take the actual exam

Take an SAT or an ACT preparatory course

In a prep course, YOU will learn helpful tips and advice for taking the SAT and the ACT.

- A prep course will familiarize YOU with the process, tests, and exam formats and sample questions.
- If a prep course is too expensive, prep books are available that are helpful as well.
- There are prep courses and prep books available for many standardized tests: SAT, GMAT, LSAT, GRE, MCAT, and others.

CHAPTER TEN

Developing a Positive Learning Attitude

Lesson #90

Be teachable

Be teachable

Why?

Teachers invest more in the students who demonstrate a desire and commitment to learning.

- Develop and exhibit a willingness to learn.
- Be open to advice.
- Allow your teacher to help YOU.
- Do what your educator asks and instructs.
- Listen to what your educators have to say.

Lesson #91

Be coachable

Be coachable

- Be coachable.
- Be open to coaching.
- Practice what YOU are taught.
- Always be open to instruction.
- Follow direction and advice on how to improve or perform better.
- Want to get better.
- Commit yourself to getting better.
- Display a positive attitude about learning, practicing, and trying new approaches and new things.
- Develop a passion for getting better at whatever YOU do.

Lesson #92

Try new things

Try new things

Why?

- Expands your perspectives on what is possible.
- Allows YOU to discover new interests.
- Helps YOU develop new skills.
- Enables YOU to discover new talents, skills, and abilities that YOU were not even aware that YOU had.

Lesson #93

Develop a love and passion for learning

Develop a love and passion for learning

Learning new things is fun, builds confidence, and enables YOU to learn more.

- Do not look at learning as a negative experience.
- Approach learning with an open mind and an open heart.
- Love to learn new things.
- Challenge yourself to enjoy the learning process.
- Never shut your mind or heart to learning something new.
- Search for new ways to learn.

Lesson #94

Always do the best that YOU can

Always do the best that YOU can

The best measuring stick is your best, not someone else's.

- Give your all each and every day, and YOU will absorb, retain, and learn more with each new experience.

- Never cheat because YOU are only cheating yourself and misrepresenting who YOU are.

Lesson #95

Be persistent

Be persistent

- Never quit because YOU are only quitting on yourself.
- Ask for help every time YOU need it, even if it feels like your educator does not want to give it to YOU.
- Believe and remember: YOU deserve the help and extra time, especially when YOU put in your best efforts daily.
- Keep working on a topic or subject until YOU understand it.
  - And yes, sometimes, YOU have to try several times before YOU truly learn it.
  - Keep practicing, trying, and working until YOU get it.

Lesson #96

Be patient with yourself

Be patient with yourself

- Recognize that YOU are not perfect, and that is a good thing.
- Do your best every day in class, on your homework, and on all essays and exams.
- Accept that mistakes are a part of learning.
- Control your emotions when YOU fail—and YOU will fail at times when YOU attempt to learn. Do not get angry. It does not imply that YOU are dumb. It simply means that YOU have a little more work to do.
- Try, try, and try again until YOU grasp the material.

Lesson #97

Keep negativity out of your mind

Keep negativity out of your mind

- Keep the voice inside your head positive.
- Even when the learning seems impossible, never give up on yourself.
- At times, others will attempt to make YOU feel bad, chastise YOU, or tease YOU when YOU commit to learning—NEVER GIVE IN TO IT!
  - If others decide not to learn, that is their problem, not yours.
- Remove "cannot" from your vocabulary.
- Refuse to say: "I cannot learn…" If YOU believe YOU cannot learn, YOU probably won't.

Lesson #98

Be positive

Be positive

- Generally, positive kids get the most help, regardless of background.
  - Think positively.
  - Act and behave positively.
  - Believe in yourself.
- Your thoughts impact your behavior, and your confidence directly impacts your ability to learn.
  - Constantly say to yourself: "I CAN LEARN!"
- If YOU truly believe that YOU can learn, YOU are much more likely to do so.

Lesson #99

Work hard to achieve success

Work hard to achieve success

"Success comes before work, only in the dictionary" so work hard. With the proper tools, time, training, and hard work, YOU CAN LEARN ANYTHING!

- Work hard.
- Work smart.
- Commit yourself to excellence.
- Be disciplined.
- Remember that there are no shortcuts to success in education or life.
- Learn and master the basics.
- Give your best effort—every time.

Lesson #100

Take control of your attitude

Take control of your attitude

- YOU control your attitude—no one else does.
  - Stay positive.
  - Look for the bright side.
  - Work hard not to let others or circumstances negatively impact your attitude.
- The better your attitude and effort are toward learning, the more help YOU will receive, the more YOU will learn, and the more YOU will get out of your education.
- Negative energy blocks your ability to think, concentrate, and absorb knowledge.
- YOU will learn more when YOU take a positive approach versus a fearful or defeated attitude.

Lesson #101

Enjoy learning

Enjoy learning

- Develop a passion for learning.
- Make it fun.
- Practice learning by reading and exploring things that interest YOU or doing things that YOU love and enjoy.
- Take pride in what YOU learn.
- Remember, the better YOU learn, the more YOU will learn and the better YOU will do in school and in life.

Lesson #102

Get selfish about your education

Get selfish about your education

- Protect it.
- Respect it.
- Do not let "friends" or peers interfere with your desire, ability, or commitment to learn.
- Make sure YOU always get something out of your educational experiences.
- Ask your family to respect your commitment to education and support YOU.

Lesson #103

*Do not fear mistakes—
they are a vital part of the
learning process*

Do not fear mistakes

- When YOU do not know how to do something, do not expect to always get it correct the first time.
- If YOU are afraid to make a mistake, YOU will rarely learn anything new.
- Mistakes do not mean that YOU are dumb. They simply mean that YOU ARE LEARNING!
- Mistakes are great teachers.
  - Find out what YOU did wrong.
  - Determine why YOU made the mistake.
  - Learn what the correct answer or process is.
  - Remember the situation/question.
  - Get it right the next time.

Lesson #104

Know that YOU can learn

Know that YOU can learn

- The four components of learning are training, tools, time, and effort.
  - Training = Being taught the basic fundamentals about a topic or subject.
  - Tools = Knowing the various formulas, procedures, formats, or processes and/or having the equipment or understanding necessary to complete a particular task successfully.
  - Time = Period of time YOU require to fully learn and understand a new concept.
  - Effort = The amount of energy, practice, discipline, and commitment YOU display to learn and understand a new concept.
- With the proper training, tools, time, and effort, YOU can learn whatever YOU desire.
- The more time and effort YOU put into anything YOU do, especially learning and education, the more successes YOU will enjoy.

Lesson #105

Know that YOU are not dumb

Know that YOU are not dumb

Pay attention to how YOU learn, even if it is not through the "traditional methods."

- There are various types of intelligence (see lesson #38).

- If YOU have problems learning, get tested to determine what help YOU need and deserve.

- If YOU are diagnosed with a learning disability, that does not mean YOU cannot learn. It simply means that YOU have to find the tools that will help YOU learn best.

- Most schools and universities are required to accommodate students with formal learning disability designations.

Lesson #106

*Think beyond yourself—
give to others*

Think beyond yourself—give to others

Doing something for someone else will make YOU feel good about yourself while adding joy to someone else's life.

- Find a way to participate in a charitable organization.
- Help someone less fortunate than YOU.
  - It will help YOU appreciate what YOU have more.
- Take pride in doing something good for someone less fortunate.
  - It will help YOU feel good about yourself.

CHAPTER ELEVEN

It Is Up to YOU!

Lesson #107

Introduce yourself to your educators and coaches

Introduce yourself to your educators and coaches

Introduce yourself to:
- Principal/head of school
- Vice principal
- Every teacher YOU have
- Librarian/coach/guidance counselor

Why?

- When people know who YOU are, they will pay more attention, especially in pivotal or critical situations.

- The more your educators know YOU care, the more likely they are to help YOU.

- YOU want to develop a rapport and relationship with these people so that if YOU ever need their help, it is much easier to communicate with them.

- When educators know what YOU are capable of, they tend to explore ways to allow YOU to showcase, improve, or share those abilities. The end result usually is improved performance or exposure for YOU.

Lesson #108

Engage in extracurricular activities that YOU like or interest YOU

Engage in extracurricular activities

Why?

- Sports, music, theater, student government, clubs, and other activities are great ways to learn, develop, and use new skills and talents.
- Extracurricular activities force YOU to organize and discipline yourself.
- Doing things that YOU like rarely feels like work.
- They give YOU an opportunity to meet people with similar interests.
- It is a great way to practice many of the new lessons that YOU are learning.

Lesson #109

Explore what YOU love

Explore what YOU love

Why?

- When YOU do what YOU love, it never feels like work.
- YOU put forth a smarter and better effort.
- Chances are the more YOU love something the better YOU will perform at it.
- YOU are less easily deterred and more committed to attaining your goals.
- When YOU do what YOU love, YOU truly enjoy yourself.
- YOU can improve your skills and abilities without negative feelings or pressure.

Lesson #110

Determine how YOU learn best

Determine how YOU learn best

When trying to remember things as YOU learn, do what works best for YOU. Which way do YOU remember things best?

- Auditory or hearing
    - Do YOU remember things better when YOU hear them or someone tells them to YOU?
- Visual or seeing
    - Do YOU remember things better when YOU see or read them?
- Kinesthetic or doing
    - Do YOU remember things better when YOU get to use your hands or learn by doing?

Lesson #111

Trust your instincts

Trust your instincts

- When YOU have properly prepared, trust the hard work YOU have put in up-front.
- Avoid second-guessing yourself.
- Trust your preparation.
  - Many times, your first instinct is accurate.

Lesson #112

Get to know yourself

Get to know yourself

The better YOU know and understand who YOU truly are the better YOU can adjust your training and approach to learning to maximize your performance.

- What do YOU like?
- What are YOU good at?
- What is hard for YOU?
- What would YOU like to be?
- What interests YOU?
- What can YOU do well effortlessly and/or naturally?
    - Explore this gift.

Lesson #113

Ask and encourage your caregivers to get involved in your education however they can

Ask your caregivers to get involved

Why?

Educators do more for YOU when they know your parents/caregivers are involved in your education.

- Ask your parents/caregivers to participate in the Parent Teacher Association (PTA).
- Ask your parents/caregivers to participate in the parent teacher conferences.
- Ask your parents/caregivers to attend your events, programs, and games.
- Share your experience and performance with your caregivers.
- Communicate!
    - Inform your caregivers of what occurs at school, what YOU are learning, and what YOU are doing.

Lesson #114

Own your performance

Own your performance

- Whether YOU learn, or not, is up to YOU.
- Whether YOU graduate, or not, is up to YOU.
- Regardless of who is teaching YOU and where YOU attend school, YOU can learn.
- Only YOU truly control your effort, desire, preparation, and commitment to learning.
- Commit yourself to always doing the very best that YOU possibly can.
- Assume full responsibility and accountability for your performance.
- Give your best effort on everything that has your name on it or that YOU are associated with—to many people, the quality of your performance reflects who YOU are.

Lesson #115

Respect yourself first

Respect yourself first

Believe in your right to learn.

- YOU deserve help.
- YOU can learn.
- YOU are not dumb.

Lesson #116

Stand on your own

Stand on your own

- Do your work.
- Respect the school, classroom, and teachers.
- Be responsible and accountable for all that YOU do.
- Again, never cheat. Do the work, and do your best.
- Earn trust by doing the right things and always being honest.

Lesson #117

Be tough and strong

Be tough and strong

- Have conviction.
- Have self-respect.
- Overcome peer pressure.
- Do not let others define who YOU are or what YOU can be.
- Develop a determination and a commitment to doing your very best at all times.
- Believe in yourself.
- YOU can do it.

Lesson #118

Become resourceful

Become resourceful

- Find ways to locate and gather important information.
- Explore options and various ways to uncover and discover facts.
- Find the truth and the facts yourself.
- Learn how to uncover the truth, facts, and important data.
- Look for great tools to help YOU learn and gather new information:
  - Internet
  - Books
  - Library
  - Other people
  - Educational television programs

Lesson #119

Let people know when YOU are doing your schoolwork

Let people know when YOU are doing your schoolwork

Ask them to help YOU learn by:

- Being quiet.
- Reading words and terms to YOU.
- Asking them to show YOU how to complete assignments.
- Allowing YOU the opportunity to teach them what YOU are learning.

Lesson #120

Take pride in everything that has your name on it

Take pride in everything that has your name on it

- Remember, it represents YOU, especially when YOU are not in the room.
- Conduct yourself with unquestionable character, dignity, and integrity.
- Take the time and care to present your school work and materials in a respectful way.
- Turn in work that is:
    - Clean
    - Neat
    - Not wrinkled or crumpled

Lesson #121

Find and use healthy stress relievers

Find and use healthy stress relievers

Find positive ways to reduce stress:
- Read.
- Listen to music.
- Play sports.
- Learn an instrument.
- Exercise.
- Meditate.
- Practice your faith.
- Get involved in community service.
- Go to the theater.
- Visit the park.
- Do something active and positive to reduce your stress.

Lesson #122

Own your education

Own your education

Getting the most out of your education is up to YOU.

- Give it your best.
- Ask for help.
- Be fully responsible and accountable for your education.
- Learn and know what is specifically required of YOU to advance or graduate.
  - Know, then verify your academic credits, grade point average, and overall standing throughout the school year.
  - Proactively, correct or address any errors in your records.
- Commit yourself to excellence, doing the very best that YOU can, and learning all that YOU can.
- Pursue your education with total commitment, effort, and focus.

Lesson #123

Communicate

Communicate

- Ask questions.
- Ask for help.
- Never be afraid to ask for help, clarification, or personal time.
- Talk, write, or e-mail your educators.
- Let people know how YOU are doing, when YOU need help, and how their help has impacted YOU.
- Share and discuss your educational experiences with others.
- Seek feedback on ways to improve.

Lesson #124

Leave "home" at home

Leave "home" at home

- Do whatever YOU can to leave the experiences of home at home.
- Focus on learning at school.
- If home is difficult, spend time at school, do your very best, and get involved in as many positive activities as YOU can handle without negatively impacting your grades.

Lesson #125

If home is particularly difficult or challenging, talk to a school counselor or adult that YOU trust about it

If home is difficult, talk to someone that YOU trust

- Do not keep the negative emotions locked inside when YOU are experiencing a difficult or challenging home situation.
    - Talking about it could provide YOU help.
    - Talking about it should help reduce some of your anxiety.
    - When YOU talk about it, YOU are no longer alone.
- When necessary, be sure to ask for help and/or advice on how to handle your situation.

Lesson #126

Use your free time at school wisely

Use your free time at school wisely

- Review your notes from that day's classes.
    - Rewrite your class notes.
    - Organize your materials from each class.
- Do your homework.
- Complete your reading assignments.
- Participate in an extracurricular activity.
- Review, organize, and update your personal calendar.
- Prepare for the next day of school.
- Begin preparing for your next test or exam.
- Review your draft essay.
- Recharge your personal battery by being with friends, relaxing, or doing something that YOU enjoy.

Lesson #127

Get involved with positive people who value education and want to learn

Get involved with positive people

- Positive people tend to have much better influences on YOU.
- Positive people tend to provide YOU with positive energy.
- YOU can learn and develop great habits from simply observing what the positive students are doing.
- Positive people tend to have higher expectations of and for themselves. That can inspire YOU to raise your own expectations.
- Positive people tend to be helpful, generous, and supportive.
- Positive people tend to want YOU to succeed.
- Positive people tend to be much happier and more fun to be around.
- Positive people tend to see the world for its boundless possibilities.
- Positive people tend to help YOU stay focused, positive, and optimistic about the future.

Lesson #128

*Take care of YOU—
body and mind*

Take care of YOU—body and mind

The better YOU take care of yourself, the more likely YOU are to be treated well by others and the more likely YOU are to treat others nicely as well.

Plus, good health directly impacts your ability to learn as well as your ability to use what YOU have learned.

Typically, the better YOU feel, the better YOU behave, think, and perform.

- Eat nutritious and healthy meals, especially on test/exam days.
- Exercise regularly.
- Get your rest and sleep on school nights. Go to bed!
- Establish a daily routine.
- Take ten minutes a day to do something that YOU love.

Lesson #129

Build lasting relationships and friendships

Build lasting relationships and friendships

YOU never know how a quality relationship developed in school will help YOU down the road.

- Make friends with your fellow students.
- Develop a bond with the teachers and coaches that help YOU and genuinely believe in YOU.
- Make positive memories and experiences with the students and teachers YOU enjoy.
- Quality relationships established at school will help YOU in more ways than YOU can imagine for the rest of your life.

Lesson #130

Have fun!

Have fun!

This is the most important part of learning:

- Enjoy yourself.
- Learn, make friends, develop new skills, but, most of all, have fun!
- Lighten up.
  - Perfection is impossible to sustain.
  - Your best is good enough.
  - Learn to forgive yourself because mistakes happen.
- Do not take yourself too seriously—laughter cures a lot of pain.
- Smile! YOU can be responsible, respectful, and committed to learning with a smile on your face.

ABOUT THE AUTHOR

Thomas Roberts epitomizes the term "people person." He has extensive experience building, leading, managing, and participating on teams in sports, community, education, and Wall Street. He loves inspiring and helping others become all that they can be.

Roberts has coached, trained, recruited, managed, taught, hired, and developed students, athletes, Wall Street professionals, and our nation's wealthiest families. He has melded the lessons, experiences, and observations from these interactions into a dynamic curriculum for all to use. His curriculum is positive, inspiring, impacting, yet simple to implement.

The content and curriculum are purely action and behavior based. They focus solely on the actions, habits, and choices that students can make that will help them to quickly become better students. His goal is to provide educational training, tips, and tools to help every individual to empower himself/herself through education.

Roberts has been a great student since his formative years at Greensboro Day School in Greensboro, North Carolina. In fact, he received the school's most prestigious award, the Founder's Award, for the graduating senior who best exemplified the school's motto: "Friendship, Scholarship, Sportsmanship."

Roberts went on to receive his BA from the College of William and Mary after successfully completing a double major in economics and anthropology in 1993. Upon graduation, he pursued a longtime dream of professional athletics by playing basketball professionally overseas in Gmunden, Austria, and Dubai, United Arab Emirates. In 2004, he received the Colonial Athletic Association's Men's Basketball Legend Award for his outstanding achievements on the floor in college and off the floor in the business world.

After retiring from basketball, Roberts began a banking career at Wachovia Bank in North Carolina. He left Wachovia to enroll in the MBA program at the Kenan-Flagler Business School at the University of North Carolina at Chapel Hill.

After graduating from the UNC Business School in 2001, Roberts moved to New York to join the J.P. Morgan Private Bank. In 2004, he left JPM to join the Citigroup Private Bank as a vice president in the firm's High Net Worth Group in Washington, DC.

Roberts retired from banking in 2006 to formally pursue his lifelong purpose and passion of inspiring, motivating, and educating others. Since retiring, he has authored two books, built three companies, and spoken to hundreds of students about the power, purpose, and possibilities that education provides. He is the founder and chief executive officer of Roberts Education Corp and the Great Student Network, a positive, collaborative, and educational support network based on Roberts' fundamental belief: "Every Student Deserves a Chance to Be Great."

Despite being the first male on either side of his family to graduate from college, Roberts has achieved tremendous success across athletics, academics, and corporate America. How did he accomplish so many things? The old fashion way—through hard work, a positive attitude, a commitment to excellence, and a relentless pursuit of education.

According to Roberts, "The only way to transcend one's current circumstances and/or to ensure that YOU maintain control over your future is through education."

Empower YOUniversity

MESSAGE AND MISSION

Empower YOUniversity is a multimedia publishing house focused on providing the educational tools and training to empower, motivate, inspire, and train YOU. Our mission is to help YOU transform your life through action-based products that are easy to use, understand, and implement in your daily life.

We recognize that YOU like to access your content in various ways, styles, and formats. Therefore, we produce our content in a variety of media formats so that YOU can choose how, and when, YOU utilize our products. Our content is not only available in traditional print format, but it will also be available in audio book, e-book, podcast, downloadable sections, CD-ROM, and DVD.

For more information, visit our website:

www.empoweryouniversitymedia.com

*"Providing YOU the Fundamentals
to Win in the Game of Life"*

HOW TO RAISE A
GREAT
STUDENT

The Ultimate Guide to
Raising the Best Student
YOU Possibly Can

THOMAS ROBERTS

HOW TO RAISE A GREAT STUDENT

How to Raise a Great Student is not just a book. It is a parent's or caregiver's:

- Personal tutor.
- Positive and helpful parental companion.
- Detailed road map for helping your child achieve success in school.
- Comprehensive resource and training guide for interacting with your child.
- Comprehensive resource and training guide for participating in your child's educational experience.
- Inspirational and motivational tool.

How to Raise a Great Student is an action-based text that is designed to help YOU become an *active* supporter of your child's educational goals. It is written in a clear, simple, and easy to understand format, use of language, and structure. Each parent point is presented on its own page and then immediately explained and reinforced on the adjacent page in order to help YOU see the message, grasp and understand it quickly, and then explain "how to use" what YOU just learned and "why" that lesson is important for YOU to know and understand. The chapters are structured specifically to help YOU prepare for your child's educational experiences.

GREAT STUDENT NETWORK

"Every Student Deserves a Chance to Be Great"

GreatStudentNetwork.com

GREAT STUDENT NETWORK

The Great Student Network is a positive collaborative member community dedicated to one fundamental belief: "Every Student Deserves a Chance to Be Great." The gateway to the network is:

GreatStudentNetwork.com

The website features educating, empowering, and inspiring information for concerned citizens, especially for students, parents, caregivers, educators, nonprofits, and socially responsible companies.

GreatStudentNetwork.com features:

- Great Student Network Awards
    - Student, Educator, and Parent/Caregiver
- Great Student Profiles
- Great Student Interviews
    - Eight Great Student Questions
- Sample Great Student Multimedia Content
    - How to Be a Great Student
    - How to Raise a Great Student
- Great Student Newsletter
- Educational Articles, Lessons, and Tips
- Sponsor Links

NOTES

NOTES

NOTES